PULP PROPHET

MCCAELA PRENTICE

Published by Musing Publications

musingpublications.com

Other works by McCaela Prentice:

Junk Drawer Heart

Pulp Prophet

by McCaela Prentice

Copyright © 2023 by McCaela Prentice

All rights reserved.

No part of this publication may be reproduced, distributed, or transmitted in any form or by any means, including photocopying, recording, or other electronic or mechanical methods, without the prior written permission of the publisher, except as permitted by U.S. copyright law. For permission requests, contact [include publisher/author contact info].

Book Cover by Finnialla Wright

1st edition 2023

To Nick, my dearest friend- my Polaris

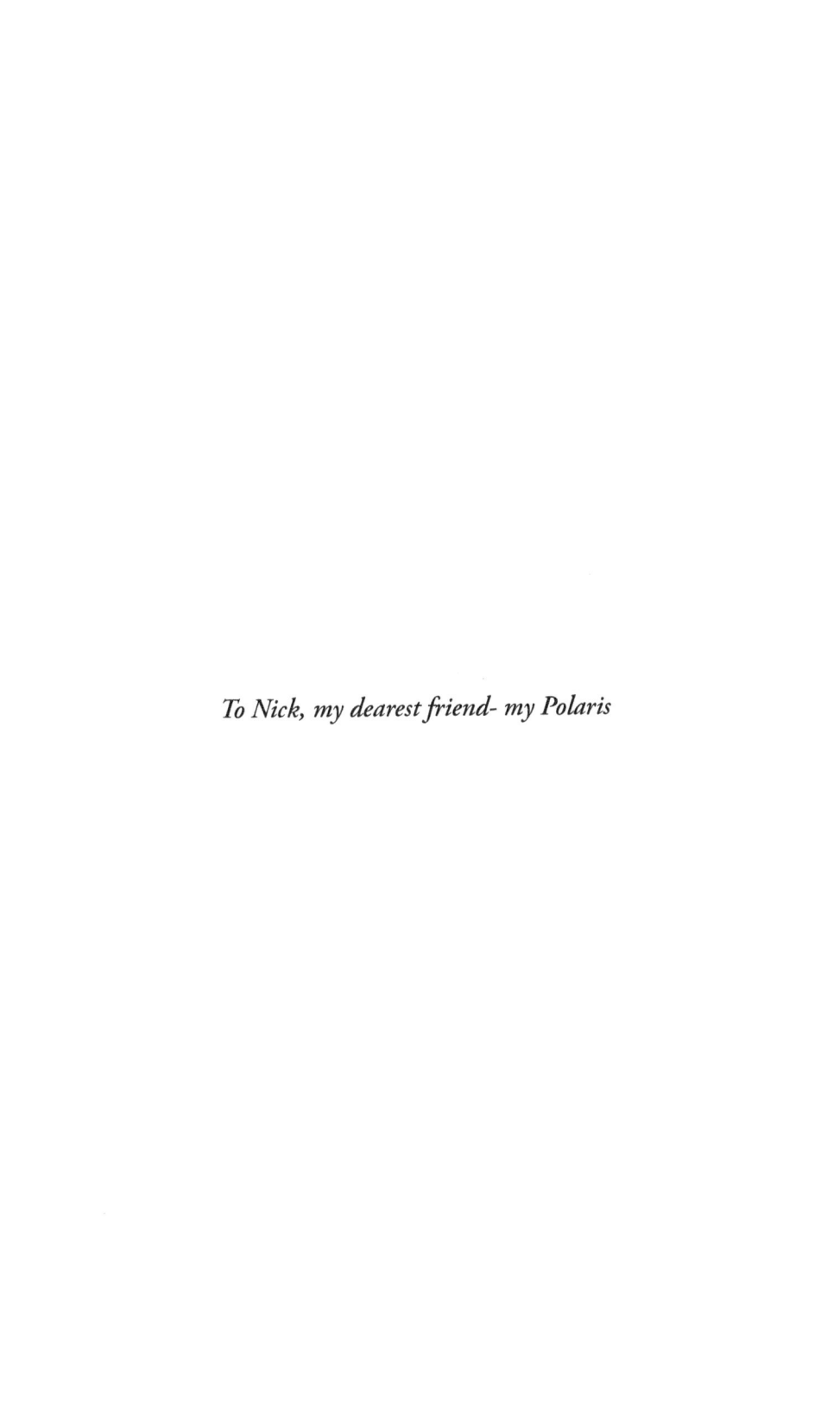

"Ah my friend, if you and I could escape this fray and live forever- never a trace of age, immortal."

-**Homer**, *The Iliad*

Contents

I. CUSP
GHOSTS TO NAME
COLLAGEN
FULL MOON PERFUME
MILK TEETH
URSA MAJOR IN THE MASON JAR
SUNBURN SANCTORUM
APOLLO AND ABSOLUTELY NOTHING
TROJAN
AFTERTASTE//AMBROSIA
LITANY AS ANOTHER MORNING IN UPPER EAST
VELVETEEN
MINIMUMS
TRACE
ON MY WALK BY THE BLOODBANK
FROGS BREATHE THROUGH THE SKIN
SURFACE TENSION
DRACO
ICARUS AND THE MERCURY YEAR
GIBBOUS

II. RETROGRADE
A STUDY OF PROMETHEUS AND WHAT WAS LEFT OF THE HARBOR
ASTORIA//RUNNING RED
SLACK JAW
LORE
YOUR POMPEII
SLEEPING SICKNESS
HYALITE

PULP PROPHET
MOMENT'S SILENCE
PERSEPHONE AND THE PULP SHE PICKED FROM HER TEETH
ON COSMIC TURNOVER, SHELLFISH, AND ENTROPY
CRUSHING LOTUS
PATROCLES//ACHILLES
MY BEST RIGHT HOOK FOR CUPID
HEARTH

III. CHART
MOON IN CANCER
SUN IN VIRGO
VENUS IN CANCER
JUPITER IN CAPRICORN
MERCURY IN LIBRA
NEPTUNE IN CAPRICORN
MARS IN CANCER
SATURN IN ARIES
PLUTO IN SAGITTARIUS
PISCES RISING

IV. MIDHEAVEN
BEACH HOUSE
DIONYSUS AND THE FULL GLASS
DELETING THE CO-STAR APP
HIVE
YOU DON'T SCARE ME
LITTLE DIPPER
NORTHERN LIGHT
POLARIS
BERGAMOT
ARACHNE AND THE LILAC TANGENT
HONEYMOON
EROS AND PULLING OUT THE ARROW
TELEGONUS AND THE DROWNING DREAMS
HERMES AND THE STORM LEVEE
ARIADNE AND THE SHIP SAILED
NIGORI SAKE AND TALKING SHIT ABOUT ZEUS
MEDUSA AND THE STONE GARDEN

Acknowledgements

I. CUSP

GHOSTS TO NAME

I do not stay with her that summer
do not fill the bird baths in the yard.
The blue jays still hover hopeful
from what collects after the rain.
I remember the rooms I cannot enter
find drawers of rusted hot wheels
and chess rooks in my secret expeditions.
The recliner by the fireplace
is worn but always empty.
She houses ghosts I want to name.
Sometimes she looks through me
calls me by another name.

COLLAGEN

the taste of copper blooms
from my tongue, it lichen splatters
on the pavement. I skin my knees
for nothing. I do not catch
the ice cream truck. I do not
wear dresses yet, do not think
how it will scar.

     I draw crude hearts
on fogged up windows in the Ford Bronco
know nothing about fossil fuels or how bad I'll be
at driving- do not fear momentums yet.

I hear it every day: the toads in the garden
will give me warts, the tree bark I grate down
will leave me marked. my legs ribboned
I thrash against my mother's arms
want to go back outside the second
the band aid is laid, my skin
peroxide bleached.

FULL MOON PERFUME

I can't find a perfume like burning cedar
and it's a shame because if I could only be reminded
at all times of dim fire and brightening skies
I may also remember seeing the moon
through a telescope for the first time
of standing in that cul-de-sac and thinking
Artemis must love me.

MILK TEETH

I thought someone might
love me by now.
I had that nightmare again -
the one where I
have forgotten my age;
have forgotten the teeth
I spit into my hands.
a boy I slept beside
told me he had dreamt it too
told me not to wish away time.

URSA MAJOR
IN THE MASON JAR

I think I'll miss the lightning bugs
next June. I'll even miss the briar
that kissed my scars crescent thin.
It was never a forever thing but I thought
the smell of pine and smoke might never
leave my flannel- that the burnt flush
of my cheeks might never be gone either.
I hate to see it fade as good things ought to;
like my best pair of jeans or a picture held
too often to the light. It's in those vanished moments -
maybe it is there you told me,
our backs sticky on the bare mattress,
about your favorite wreath of stars
and why old gods hung it there.
you were wrong to say it was an act of love -
the flies in the jar and Callisto in his sky.
drifting follows heavy and horizon promises
no fixed constellations- a world just cruel enough
to let me have you one last time.

SUNBURN SANCTORUM

the wasps will nest where they are not welcome.
under the lattice or along the roof where we
pour mead and feel like Midas in the first hour
looking sundown blush and hard at nothing.

I will only be golden while my skin is flush
with my baked blood- while I wear my warmest
shade of eyeshadow. come dusk I'll hang over
the fire escape- I'll melt into ozone and catch
your smoke rings by their helix.

APOLLO AND ABSOLUTELY NOTHING

nothing has to wait until the weekend.

I'll send you the photo and lay down
in the AC. I want to walk home with gelato
running down my forearms and bitch
about the heat.

I want you to hurry.

TROJAN

boy at the brewery
folds me an origami horse;
I fold myself over another boy
in the parking lot that night.

next week I will take nothing
will not leave my necklace on the dash
will think nothing of the canyon between me
and his bloodied back

where the crimson quiet is all that we
sleep off. if it's rivers he wants,
if it's things that run
then I'll be gone soon.

AFTERTASTE // AMBROSIA

The morning she died I must have been
still swimming— the taste of Aperol
still roosting on my tongue

must have been breathing life
into some clay- heavy man
or licking out a candle wick

and telling the good lie
that I like the drinks neat;
that no matter the arson
I will stay.

LITANY AS ANOTHER MORNING IN UPPER EAST

the dead do not visit me in dreams -
must remember I do not listen. I am certain
I've kicked off the sheets when I wake to you
and the linen landing on me gently.
when I go, I hold you a little
too long, kill the headache with a coffee
on my walk home. I think of you in church,
think of you saying my name like a prayer -
peel the skin off my lip and wonder
if you sleep better with me gone.

VELVETEEN

It's Pisces season and so I
find the cheapest bottle of red
leave ruby rings on your glass table,
a deep purple in my throat.

I want my voice to feel like velvet
want to be remembered the way
that you remember all the words
to Billy Joel songs. I have never
seen a live performance I did not
feel religion for. I have never
brushed lips with anything worth
dying for - which is not to say
I have not tried.

MINIMUMS

I am reminded by the radio/ by a chariot across the sky/ that
youth is but a blaze and I/ am but a stardust-spattered lush/
up on a barstool. I'm so sick of kissing/ soured mouths
wondering if you're single now/ if somebody
is loving you/ the way I used to/ if it is

less than/ greater than/ equal to

it's all that orbits my skull/on my walk home/losing count
of the stars/tugged magnetic north/and how does that song go?
the one where she/says heaven is all for you/has been here
all along/is an eyelash wish-honey/is it true?/ is infinity
a minimum? in the morning maybe/I'll call you/tell you I
dreamed
of monarch migrations again/of the unquantifiable.

TRACE

The days now leave me
short of breath. A man is edging along
a guard rail on the Queensboro bridge.
I have only ever seen the bedroom
dimly lit. I have only walked here once.
I drag my finger along the yellow line
for a stranger on the train.
these are places I have been;
places my time has traced.
I get lost on my way home
from the bar in west but know
the new decade that waits
like lipstick on the mirror;
that in it you wake to find
your hands spotted
over and over again.

ON MY WALK BY THE BLOOD BANK

I think of collapsed veins, of flumes and running water
the redwoods funneled down some nightmare channel,
corpses carried miles from their ghost; empty saw mills
and how the dust settles so fine. I do not know my blood type -
the arteries or artifice that carry me through the self..
I cannot wrap my arms around the base of a sequoia -
around the man when he tells me it took them
twelve hours to retrieve the body. I do not pretend to know
the swallows of that grief- do not dwell on a future
where it will swallow me. I see the bags stacked red and think
of sap – think of Ichor and how viscous are our losses.

FROGS BREATHE THROUGH THE SKIN

like frost heaves gasp
for air through cracked pavement.

                          it's another cruel spring
back home- the spring peepers chorus buried by a late sheet
of ice.

                every April I unlearn it:
the rise and fall of my chest. every date is just *before*
or *after* .

                my eyes stay tadpole round
and bog dry. I think I could sleep almost anywhere now.

on the riverbank soft and sinking; in that cold water with
my fingers webbed.

                I had begged to become laurel
to become nothing at all. to wade into all my undoings

but no intervention
is so divine.

SURFACE TENSION

I cannot shake a certainty
of sea serpents

even after all this time
and all the waters that have
I think now only spared me

or have only just begun
to consider me a meal and not
a thing in motion.

I always thought that would be the way.
cold water, gnashing teeth;

churned waters
in the way of mercy.

DRACO

the water rises and takes
the contour of a serpent -
of someone I have known.
draco was my favorite
constellation I could never find.
some things you are born into -
shedding skins; a golem tide.
I have been looking
in all the wrong places.
It couldn't be scales
budding under my bruised knees;
It couldn't be that I
have washed up here again.
I always thought I'd have
some other life- some other body
to coil around.

ICARUS AND
THE MERCURY YEAR

It's not true what they say
about timing- about getting pulled
into the orbit of something that burns brighter.

I am learning about gravities- that it would have been
a year on Mercury. that I would be half my age on
Mars.

I have called all things I get close to
the Sun. I get it now, Icarus and his matrimony
to the sky- the heat death of the universe;

the slow burn of us. the horizon swears
infinity but I watch the sun
sink somewhere.

GIBBOUS

there is no meteor shower,
no occasion for the smoke
that blows back in
my window. the skyline
is insatiable. I have known
the stars as proof of ghosts;
lipstick as proof of other.
I cannot compromise
on this- I have seen him
cast the glow of past lives.
I too have waned
and waxed with it -
have looked up and hoped
no one was looking back.

II. RETROGRADE

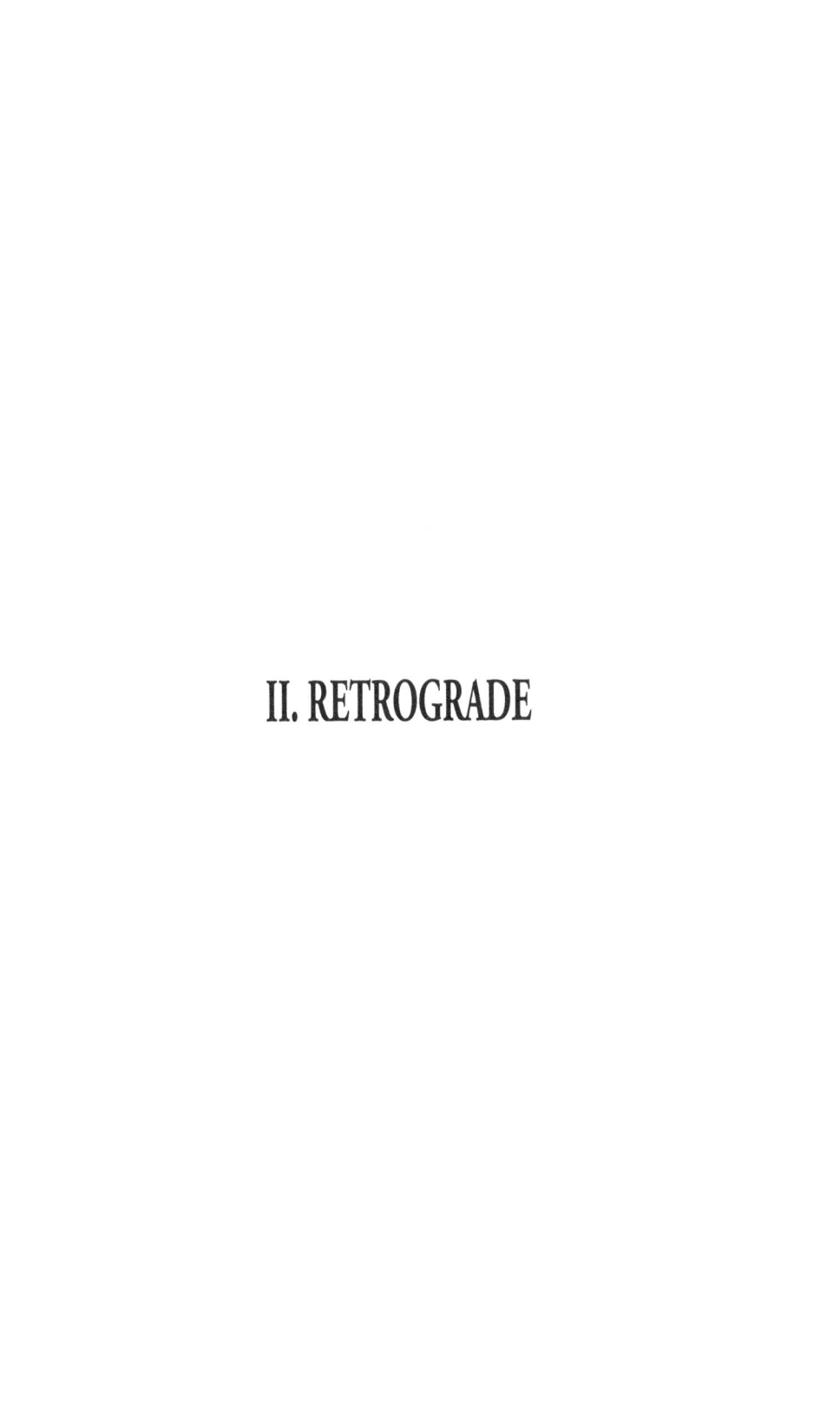

A STUDY OF PROMETHEUS AND WHAT WAS LEFT OF THE HARBOR

I. I cannot mistake it for love,

the clay beneath the nails and the sun crashing
into the day with the familiar ferocity of the last

for every morning I saw him grin
wide as Bass Harbor
knowing what came next

II. It's your best trick

to throw me up against the countertop
like I'm a fire you must put out

and then only watch yourself
in the mirror

III. I've walked hotter coals

to convince myself it was
something I'd been given;

a sacrifice, all so I
could walk home bruised
and buy my favorite flowers

IV. for nothing

I've driven to that shore and looked up
at that cliff

to see the raptors dancing on the dying beams
of sunlight sinking

into my dark reflection

V. again

my fingers feel that they are burning
and I flinch

when you kiss my stomach.
I think now forever

is a threat.

ASTORIA // RUNNING RED

you look strange late day-
I don't remember you so well.

someone that looked more like you
heard the sirens hail the city-

bit their tongue clean through,
forgot tying cherry stems

or anything so cruel as mouths.
ask me about blood loss

about the sluggish trickle
of the Lethe-

how I drank from it
to unknow you like a dream.

SLACK JAW

I can't close my mouth around your tide
or the whale shark eclipsing the sun

It gets dark too early now for me
to chase you up the Meridian
and over Atlas;

up all of my imagined halves
and crystallized arches

I've always wanted an imaginary friend like you-
have always wanted to suck up the ocean
through a paper straw

to drool onto my pillow and wake up glad
the sun burned up my blinds

LORE

what is a word if I pick it apart
like hot wax off my hands?

who are you if I keep reinventing you
every time you spend the night -

if I keep making and unmaking us?

let's say lore. let's say it over and over
until our tongues are numb and there's nothing
left but soot.

the benadryl makes me feel like I could slip
through the earth's mantle- makes me feel like there
might never be another spring.

he came up on a chariot; he came up through the bedrock.

no, he came in through the window with a bottle of Heineken
and said he couldn't live without.

he said it over and over
until it was lore. until it was nothing.
until it was a cup of water
emptied on my bed.

YOUR POMPEII

It's fire season and I want to be a better god; to be your pompeii
but one morning I was not myself. I will tell you a secret-
I will tell you what the arsonist told me as he struck the match
against his teeth. that all those who create are the god
of something small- that the bed is once again a pyre
and my body an offering. I want to burn up in something-
want to be sage sweet and better with my hands
but the rivers still don't bend for me; the heavens not a candle wick
for me. I will tell you what I saw that night- the heat lightning
and the shadow in the doorway. that I woke with ash beneath my nails.
that I went out to find the snow had turned pumice gray-
how I watched it fall all around me.

SLEEPING SICKNESS

In my sleep I suppose a haunting-
say I doubt the boundaries of our bodies
but what I mean is every night I unearth an old fear
that there is nothing between us.

so often is a ghost just someone I'm about to miss-
is a man I've held sleeping with his back to me.
I don't miss the mornings I was invisible-
that I didn't wake up from the bad dream
where hands flay me like fever but my face
is someone else's.

HYALITE

bad luck to wear opal
if it's not your birthstone-
my birthright is to petrify.

I have found myself
wishing my eyes serpentine
green like the bottom
of an algae conquered pool
between sun ripples- wishing I
could hold anything so well
as limestone or a gaze.

I have gained nothing
in this gift but cessation
and lifetimes of it. I will collect
the years like rings of trees -
know them by the cracks
weeping down my masonry.

PULP PROPHET

I dream prophecy and forget the warning
upon waking- some nagging thought
that feels like paper dropped in water
screams itself void as I sit up.

It's just a day;
it's just a feeling
that I should not take the long walk.

I wonder did Cassandra
ever doubt her gift and will I ever
wake up feeling right

steadied by the arm around me,
the cool quilt pushed aside
so carefully for

all passion is kinetic
is just motion with the heaviness
of pulp.

at all times I am
waiting on inertia;
am waiting to say
I saw it coming.

MOMENT'S SILENCE

damn the false start-
the magnolias have come too soon
their petals like beads of broken rosary
clung to the wet pavement.
the rain, the pulp of it between my fingers
are no remedy for what has gone-
my mouth no more;
that season no longer.

PERSEPHONE AND THE PULP
SHE PICKED FROM HER TEETH

I will not make a myth of you- of the limestone
and calcites dripping

like the red juice down my chin. I loved you
so bad. it eclipsed the longest day.

it made the sky swallow itself
like ouroboros in a vernal pool.

maybe I will never see another star;
maybe I will never know a greater grief

than the one that eats in circles -

that leaves the petals crushed
and nails bloodied against granite.

ON COSMIC TURNOVER, SHELLFISH AND ENTROPY

The universe is at all times
moving toward a state of chaos

that's what I know   from thermodynamics
      from how I use my phone so carelessly
all weekend,

dialing your number and using his bed
      as a lifeboat- universal law says
      energy

goes nowhere and so even if
I drown,
      even if isopods
      on the seafloor carry me
miles from myself,
      I will somehow be
still here.

In the same way I may be
      nothing new. I may have been
a soft shell crab
      or Thetis
dangling a boy of borrowed time
and carbon by his heel.

I think too much   about where to end.

maybe then death is just a return to self -
maybe then
      in answering your call I am returning
      to a self that died.

it could be all these plated crabs   are just
people that will be   again. that after dinner

    they will roll exhausted
    into the next existence

and that so will I.   that I may find myself
submerged; my heel wriggling
just above the surface of the water.

CRUSHING LOTUS

After life maybe there will be
halves of me unfinished

like the cut pomelo
on the park bench
in Tompkins Square

maybe it will be
like the first minutes of waking -
thoughts of nothing but the light
burning through my blinds.

PATROCLES // ACHILLES

I am carved up by the dull knife
of a stupid man. I knew it already
that the hero's journey is gilded
dogshit.

please don't worry. please don't go
out in the armor. It should be enough

to be loved. they launched
a thousand ships for less.

MY BEST RIGHT HOOK FOR CUPID

Cupid is getting lazy and you are getting sunburnt
on the tapestry we've laid out in the park. you say it's lucky
red is my favorite color. that maybe then I'll love you
as much as blush— as much as sangria in the place
of water or as anything that makes me dizzy. It's agony,
isn't it? That warm things can hurt us; that one day a freckle
on my skin may be more than just a solar kiss. that one day I will
box your things carefully and that it will feel the same
as the times before. so careful is the routine of departure
and so lonely is the intimacy shared with a man who
performs acts of devotion only for the self. that you may
mistake him for kind— that you may crown him
with sweet nights and wake to put the blanket
over him. that I may look up at red skies
and think only how lovely he might look
in that violent light

HEARTH

I am left hearth warm with a blanket
between my legs. you kissed me too hard
beneath the sumacs but still, I stayed.
I was told there is no love without
great sacrifice and what more,

what more could I surrender?
our hands were pressed together
so tight I thought
it was a prayer.

there was such a severity
between us. so often in the night
you clung to me like sheets of ivy
that I mistook the desperation
for urgency, and dare I say
desire.

III. CHART

MOON IN CANCER

I have felt all the things and washed
my hands of them- have moved the letters
from my nightstand. your handwriting
is shit.

SUN IN VIRGO

I can stand to witness you -
to see you approach my door
empty handed just as I
remembered you.

VENUS IN CANCER

I had kissed you like a river's mouth
and watched you tumble brackish
into another body -
into a softer tide

JUPITER IN CAPRICORN

I believed in willow-the-wisps
and for a lesser time
that I could love us both
through anything.

MERCURY IN LIBRA

I promised you
a way back. that I might flicker in
like candlelight and melt
over the edge of your bed

NEPTUNE IN CAPRICORN

In a dream I danced with you
on Orion's belt- told you the waves
all looked like lemon meringue and that I
would fetch a fallen star for you

MARS IN CANCER

I owe you more severity. It was so unkind
of me to let you sleep against me
while all night I felt the words
start cutting at my throat

SATURN IN ARIES

I look back at nothing now.
one day I cleaned the closet
and found the box collecting dust
so evenly.

PLUTO IN SAGITTARIUS

You always found new ways to tell me
I'm not fixed- that the sunken space
on my side of your mattress
would take shapes like water.

PISCES RISING

I only took your word for it -
licked knives like rims of glass
so that you might love me darker
than what bled from me.

IV. MIDHEAVEN

BEACH HOUSE

I did not see the whale breach the water
but here we are talking about Gods again.
the cirrocumulus clouds today at least look viperine -
look like a thing with its legs spread. we should salt the windows

or burn a candle all the way through. I'm waiting for a wave
to hit me so hard I bioluminesce. we should overwater all
the house plants - we should get sand in the sheets and
sleep in them anyways.

it would rub the skin on my legs smooth -
you have rubbed my chin raw as thirst
but I have since forgotten
the ache that is waking
to your hand in mine.

DIONYSUS AND THE FULL GLASS

we kill the bottle of honey wine in the warm light
and see how it looks like sunshine or a mosquito
trapped in amber when we hold it just above our heads.
we agree most good things are stolen.
like myths and kisses. I know the feeling
of getting home in the early hours and dreaming
yourself through the whole next day- an aching
head and the memory like a photo negative
of legs over the covers. laughing as the glass ran over
and you wouldn't stop pouring. the rings like Saturn's
where our cups stuck to the table into the next
blue morning.

DELETING THE CO-STAR APP

If I were a siren I'd crash your boat best
and turn off my push notifications.

the Co-Star app says I should try
not drowning today

says the best part about the ocean
is what is lost there

says something about watching out
for rising tides and men that search

the beach for shark teeth. that we
are as compatible as Odysseus' ship

and the rocks of Scylla which is just
another way of saying the love would

eat one of us alive when the other
wasn't looking— is just another way

I quiet those swimming desires and kiss
them over like a shipwreck; that I am still

at the mercy of the currents
that pull me back to you.

HIVE

I.

most nights I am glad he's gone

am glad I get to keep my nights
and sleeping murmurs all my own.

II.

I will keep all the secrets
that dripped from your tongue

will hold them
like a grudge

or like a hand pulling me
from the density of my dreams

III.

do you sleep better now

am I so restless even
in the quiet hours

and would you
have liked me better still?

IV.

I thought of something
but it can wait.

YOU DON'T SCARE ME

the way perfusion does; in the way of loam
and insects prying at my eyelids. I know
better than to run with shears but this
can't wait- the pruning of the wild
thing within me. we agree that there
were moments.

that they were only moments. when I wake
with dirt beneath my nails I think it must mean
hands reaching from the earth and you buried
before I had the chance to tell you
the truth in it- that love doesn't move
like that. that you can't bury the living.
believe me, I have tried.

LITTLE DIPPER

ladle that dark into my mouth

and maybe it will taste

like honey or like lobster bisque

will be so dense on my tongue that I

will barely be able to lift it

when I say to you

I saw the closing of the hands

each night around the sun

and that it did not feel like love

to be held only for the sake

of being hidden

NORTHERN LIGHT

I would like to see them once before I die
or better yet to swim through them when I do.

I could see it then awash in green- everything
for what it was:

the hand of my friend dragging me down a
busy street so drunk the street lights

were a great inferno- the shortness of my breath
as we laughed so hard we snuffed out Polaris.

the skies a swell of absinthe and your clothes covering my
floor.

the salvation in that brief acuity
of your sharp inhale.

POLARIS

I am grateful for the north I knew
and for the empty lumen of my heart
echoing the cries of hermit thrush
like a morning made brittle by
a late sun.

I used to drag the constellation book
into your bed. do coal-powered stars
grant wishes? Is it still there -
the blanket of moss stretching static soft
on that balding mountain?

I want to be known now -
I want to feel it
beneath my palms.

BERGAMOT

in my dreams I am searching always for fiddleheads
to pluck from the moss like harp strings. someone is there
and I think that they must love me

because they warn me, wordlessly,
of ground hornets and of bergamot cologne
seeping into the carpet while I'm away

I am aware of an allergy (mine or theirs)
when I wake with hands sore from
crawling all that earth and I want

to keep everything alive
but I fill my basket.

ARACHNE AND THE LILAC TANGENT

I lay the lavender sprigs out uneven
and think the smell is just like where the milkweed
sprouted feathers and the monarchs

set themselves and the graying coast ablaze -
how spring at home is always a lilac tangent
and how that same purple spins itself
like an arachnid into the fibers of the spitting
winter skies.

I would be a better weaver if I believed
in precision- if I believed myself to be
a master of my body.

I grip the lantern my whole walk home.
I think of threading the needle.

HONEYMOON

everything smells like honeysuckle
at the wedding and I think what it must be
to love like leaving a tab open
or a thrown bouquet that will not
hit the ground.

at the open bar all of the drinks have clove—
have the taste of a summer I am lucky
to have lived through. A man tells me
he can't stop thinking about Sisyphus—
says in all his dreams the halls are inclined.

we agree that all things eternal
are damnation but I keep thinking of the dress
with red wine spilled on white sheets
and the honeymoon.

EROS AND PULLING OUT THE ARROW

I pull you into me like a drawstring

and exhaust my resistance. by the street lights
I think I catch you smile.

I don't think it's love I just think it's
the lighting. painted gold you look so

prophetic- look sun streaked
and mirage steady.

I wish it were as easy as an arrow notched.
I wish in bringing you the aloe
I meant nothing but

I dread to know what would drip
from my pierced heart

and more to know
what might not
drip from yours

TELEGONUS AND THE DROWNING DREAMS

It feels wrong. The comforter too hot for November
and the way you look at me too long when I
tell you it is crushing- when I tell you yesterday I woke up at 3
PM, still tired and then not to look at me at all.

I've been wanting to tell you something but it keeps leaving me
like a dream- too quickly to miss. It's just that sometimes I feel
concurrent- feel like Telegonus standing on the beach

feel far from here but when I close my eyes
my feet are buried by sand the color of milk in earl grey
and you are squinting at me in the sun. It can't be nothing
that I dream of you. It can't be nothing that in the dreams of you

we are mourning something by the water -
that you are telling me stories about drowning while we swim.

I wonder too if all I need to love you is to cross
an ocean. is to wake up early and kiss you
harder than the cold spray
of the sea.

HERMES AND THE STORM LEVEE

everyone is busy. everyone is in love.

I am licking the envelope. In the letter
I confess

I have searched everywhere. I have started
to use the bookmark.

I have been window shopping
and seeing us on storm levees.

how can it be
an ocean between us?

how can it be
that there are so many floods when you
are none of them?

ARIADNE AND THE SHIP SAILED

before we fell asleep I thought about what held up the moon.
invisible string and someone walking it like a puppeteer into
the sun's glare- arms like yours holding it high above your
head and casting it down when they tire. I thought of pulling
tides and what a relief it might be if I made you up entirely.
In that liminal space between skyline and shore. with the
water ripped back.
seafoam or heaven.

you said once I'd look fit to kill
in red or in unraveling threads. you said once
whatever sank the ship was the color
that my eyes were.

how could you? how could you have me
storm gray and so raptured- pressed so hard
to every surface?

you said sometimes it was
like you couldn't breath- that your hands
just found my throat.

NIGORI SAKE AND TALKING SHIT ABOUT ZEUS

it's no wonder the gods drank. I wonder if they

could remember everything.

I can't remember
what sake

we ordered or telling you
that story.

what was I ever mad about?

what was it the glass
broke over?

my hand felt like it was breaking.

I don't wish I could remember
everything;

my hand felt like it was breaking.

MEDUSA AND THE STONE GARDEN

I dozed off in the garden
with my belly full of stones.
they went down easy and I hope the vines
keep growing and that time eats all
the men that came here to leave heroes -
that time may steal their contour
like water evaporating from the bird bath.
It's not monstrous to wish it; to sleep just
a moment longer. I've been having the dream where
I hold the sword. I've been having the dream where
I am the sword and the cuts bleed amber,

that color like foliage- the color of something
gone for good. I think sometimes in seasons.
I think sometimes hero
is just whoever holds the sword
is whoever wants a trophy bad enough
to leave the garden razed. I will decorate them
in creeping ivy. I will say green is a more
forgiving color.

ACKNOWLEDGEMENTS

I am so very grateful to the editors and staff of the following publishers for sharing my work:

Detritus Online: "LITANY AS ANOTHER MORNING IN UPPER EAST"

Perhappened Mag: "A STUDY OF PROMETHEUS AND WHAT WAS LEFT OF THE HARBOR"

Twist in Time Mag: "MILK TEETH"

Giallo: "BEACH HOUSE"

Gastropoda: "HONEYMOON" and "LITTLE DIPPER"

The Jupiter Review: "DIONYSUS AND THE FULL GLASS"

Superfroot Mag: "YOU DON'T SCARE ME"

Wind Up Mice: "SUNBURN SANCTORUM"

The LA Review: "ON MY WALK BY THE BLOOD BANK"

Mineral Lit: "MINIMUMS"

"McCaela Prentice's debut collection, PULP PROPHET, holds the same electric charge felt when you enter a room and know you are about to witness something you won't be able to forget. These bright and lyrical poems trace a series of thin lines between nostalgia for youth and impatience to emerge into maturity or doubt: 'I mistook the desperation / for urgency, and dare I say / desire' Shock me, these poems seem to ask all while knowing they, like Cassandra, have seen it all coming before. Prentice's vividness and allusions flow through this collection like remnants of prophecy, ensuring damage and dissatisfaction that edges the catwalk of the Queensboro bridge, or comes through the window with memories 'like a photo negative / of legs over the covers.' Be careful, they warn, for certainty is the snake holding its tail, shedding skin after skin, to reveal itself again."

-Jared Beloff, author of *Who Will Cradle Your Head*

Pulp Prophet is an enchanting collection of poems that explores Greek mythology, aging anxiety, and oversleeping in all its complexities. With its evocative imagery and lyricality, this collection delves deep into the intricacies of human emotions and relationships. From the alluring yet dangerous Sirens to the tragic fate of Icarus, Pulp Prophet uses these timeless myths as a lens to view the struggles and triumphs of modern life. Through the mythologizing of a breakup and the unraveling of the self - like the thread in the labyrinth of the minotaur - these poems take us on a journey of self-discovery and introspection.

McCaela Prentice (she/her) is living and writing in Astoria, NY. She awaits the Percy Jackson renaissance. Her poems have previously appeared in HAD, Ghost City Review, and Perhappened. Her debut chapbook *Junk Drawer Heart* was published in 2020 by Invisible Hand Press.

Published by Musing Publications

musingpublications.com

Cover design: Finnialla

ISBN 979-8-218-18943-3

Printed in the USA
CPSIA information can be obtained
at www.ICGtesting.com
LVHW091744011023
759753LV00007B/685